INDIAN ARTS

BY THE SAME AUTHOR
THE INDIAN AND HIS HORSE
THE INDIAN AND THE BUFFALO
INDIAN BEADWORK
INDIAN COSTUMES
INDIAN FISHING AND CAMPING
INDIAN GAMES AND CRAFTS
INDIAN HUNTING
THE INDIAN MEDICINE MAN
INDIAN MUSIC MAKERS
INDIAN PICTURE WRITING
INDIAN SIGN LANGUAGE
INDIAN WARRIORS AND THEIR WEAPONS
INDIANS AT HOME
INDIANS ON THE MOVE
THE INDIAN'S SECRET WORLD

G.W.

INDIAN ARTS

WRITTEN AND ILLUSTRATED BY

ROBERT HOFSINDE
(Gray-Wolf)

WILLIAM MORROW AND COMPANY
NEW YORK

ACKNOWLEDGMENTS

The author wishes to express his thanks to Mr. Myles Libhart, Director of Museums, Exhibitions, and Publications, United States Department of the Interior, Indian Arts and Crafts Board, for permission to adapt drawings from the Board's official photographs. The author further thanks Dr. Frederick Dockstader, Director of the Museum of the American Indian, New York City, for permission to make drawings from the museum's collection.

United States Department of the Interior, Indian Arts and Crafts Board, 17; 18; 21; 23 top and bottom; 25 center; 27 bottom left; 31 top; 69; 71; 87

United States Department of the Interior, Indian Arts and Crafts Board, Southern Plains Indian Exhibit and Crafts Center, Anadarko, Oklahoma, from mural "A Successful Raid" by Allan Houser, 85

United States Department of the Interior, Indian Arts and Crafts Board, from mural "Apache Women Gossiping" by Allan Houser, 80

Museum of the American Indian, 25 bottom; 28; 31 bottom; 32; 35; 37; 39; 46; 67 bottom left

Pipestone National Monument, Pipestone, Minnesota, 45 (L-shaped pipes)

All other drawings made from the author's private collection.

To the Indian artist
of long ago, of today, and of tomorrow,
I sincerely dedicate this book.

CONTENTS

INDIAN ARTS

1

EARLY INDIAN ART

The Indian's desire to record events taking place around him resulted in artistic expression. In the earliest days, he scratched designs on birchbark scrolls and told his story on tanned buffalo robes and tepee walls. He also painted symbolic figures on stone cliffs.

Perhaps kneeling on a river raft, the Northern Indians decorated the rock walls, often beneath an overhanging ledge, where their work would be shielded from sun and rain. These early artists made their pigments from iron-bearing rock minerals, which they ground to a fine powder and mixed with animal fat or fish oil. The color was a deep red, and it lasted permanently.

In what is now Canyonlands National Park, in Utah, the Indians cut petroglyphs into cliffs that had a smooth, dark crust of iron and manganese oxide. Their tools most likely were made from hard stones or antler points. The crowded designs showed animals, people, birds, and trees. There also were circles within circles and uneven lines, which may have represented snakes or perhaps crooked trails.

Throughout the North American continent, cliffs and rock walls decorated with paintings still can be found. Even in their crude form we can recognize prehistoric animals.

Cliffs rising from waters all through the canoe routes in northern Minnesota show many pictographs as clearly as when they first were painted. Throughout the Southwest other cliff paintings can

be seen, including those at Canyon de Chelly and Canyon de Muerto in the Navaho country of Arizona. Some are pre-Columbian, while others are a mere 150 years old. Many of them are best viewed from horseback, since they are a distance from the ground.

Due to their antiquity we only can conjecture about the significance of these art forms. Perhaps they had ceremonial meanings or were personal or tribal records of important deeds. Or they might have been symbols explaining the dreams and visions from the spirit world to one seeking his dream totem in the solitude of the cliff.

Through the years, the Indian artist gained more skill. His figures of animals became more lifelike and better proportioned, although they remained abstract in design.

About a thousand years ago, when the Pueblo Indians began to use adobe for the walls of their structures, the tribal artists found that this material provided an ideal background for their work. They began to create large murals on the walls of the kivas, the underground ceremonial chambers that existed in every village. By means of slow and painstaking work, archeologists have been able to restore some of them.

The mural shown in the drawing of the kiva interior was discovered in Arizona, in 1938. The illustration with the three figures on the next page was painted in the sixteenth century, and it shows clearly the continuity of Pueblo culture. The mask on the middle figure is similar to those that Hopi kachina dancers wear today. Hopi Indians also wear the same type of belt, as well as the kilts and sashes on the smaller figures. The original meaning of these murals

is unknown, although they surely must have been
of a religious nature.

Whatever their meaning, these artistic forms were
a means of preserving the ancient lore in much the
same way that it was kept alive through legends,
songs, dances, and ceremonials.

The Indian's skill in his early paintings is also
evident in many of the things he made for his everyday use, his ceremonial life, as well as for hunting
and warfare. The following chapters will discuss
some of the Indian arts and describe how he created
many useful and decorative items from a variety of
materials.

2

HORN, BONE, SHELL, AND QUILL

The different tribes used natural materials to make a number of objects. Some were native to the region where the tribe lived, while others were obtained through trade.

Many substances came from animals, such as antelope and buffalo, which lived on the prairie, although buffalo existed as far south as Georgia until about 1860. Deer also were found in most states. Other materials included shells, such as dentalium, cowrie, and abalone, which were gathered along the coast and traded to the inland peoples. The Plains Indians used quills, which they secured from the woodland tribes.

The Sioux and the Blackfeet made spoons from buffalo and sheep horns with tools of flint, bone, and sandstone. First the craftsman placed the horn in a fire to burn out all the fatty tissue. Then he put it into boiling water until it became soft and pliable. Next he trimmed the broad part of the horn to form the spoon bowl, and, if necessary, he bent the tapered end to the desired curve.

While the horn was still soft, he placed a stone of the proper size and shape into the bowl and secured it with a wrapping of buckskin. Then he set the spoon aside to harden. After it had cooled, the Indian smoothed the entire spoon with a piece of sandstone. He polished it to a high gloss by rubbing animal fat into it.

These tribes rarely carved their spoons, but ornamented them with a band of fine quillwork. To use

the tubular quills, first they were flattened. Even a tool for this simple work had decorations. The Blackfeet made a quill flattener from a carved and incised antler or from a buffalo horn.

The style of quillwork applied to the handle was called plaiting in which the woven quills formed diamond shapes. With a background of the natural white quill, plus two or three differently colored dyed quills, the decoration stood out in fine contrast to the natural blackness of the horn.

Some Sioux medicine men used carved and pierced antelope horns, decorated with brass-headed nails, as a part of their medicine bundle.

The Northwest Coast Indians made spoons and ladles for daily household use from sheep horns, which were long and curved. The bowl of the spoon was inserted into a separate handle. The handles were highly carved with intricate designs, and often they were inlaid with pieces of abalone shell.

For use during a potlatch, a large family feast, these Indians made serving ladles from mountain-sheep horns, which often measured fifteen inches in

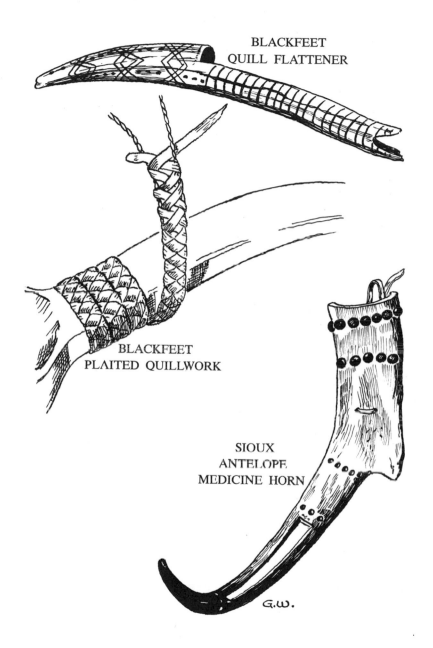

BLACKFEET
QUILL FLATTENER

BLACKFEET
PLAITED QUILLWORK

SIOUX
ANTELOPE
MEDICINE HORN

G.W.

length. A typical one had a handle in the shape of a king salmon, and its bowl was decorated with an incised design.

Many of their carving tools were formed out of jade. This stone is very hard, and it can take and hold a sharp edge.

Some Indians made decorative items from animal bones. From the early sixteenth century well through the eighteenth, those in the Eastern woodland areas, principally the Iroquois, skillfully carved bone combs from flat bone sections, such as the shoulderblade of the deer.

First the craftsman boiled the bones in water to rid them of all fat. Then he left them in the open air to dry and bleach. He formed the long, slender teeth by cutting into a bone with a sharp, flat stone. Then he rubbed them smooth with a piece of sandstone. The Indian decorated the upper half of the comb with carvings representing birds, people, or animals. The illustrated carving of the fighting bears is a fine example of early Iroquois work.

The woodland as well as the prairie tribes made

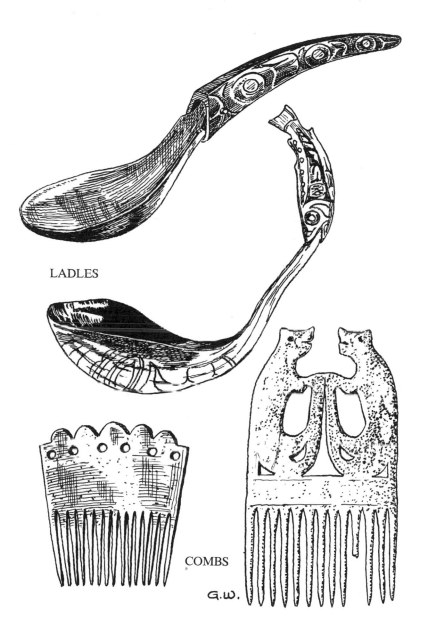

LADLES

COMBS

G.W.

a head ornament known as a roach from the hairs of a deer's tail. It stood erect, like a crest, on the warrior's head from his brow to the nape of his neck. The center of the roach had a flat base, which was broad in front and tapered to a point at the back.

To keep the roach hairs in a vertical position, an ornamental spreader was tied on top of the base at its broadest part. Usually it was made from a flat piece of bone with one or two bone tubes fastened on it. These served as sockets to hold the upright feathers. The spreader on the left is of Sioux make, while the one on the right is Ojibwa.

The Indians used shells of various kinds for decoration. The Northwest Coast people formed borders or designs on their blankets with dentalium shells. They made necklaces with cowrie shells and ornamented the fringe of their costumes and dresses with them.

Prehistoric Indians of Tennessee and nearby states made shell gorgets, or breast ornaments. Both men and women wore them. It is thought that they were a symbolic badge of tribal or religious authority.

ROACH

ROACH
WITH SPREADER

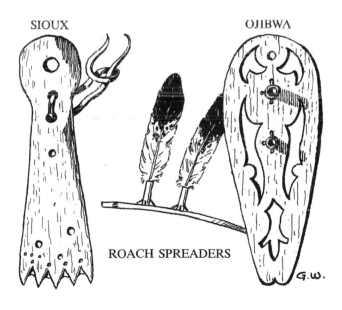

SIOUX

OJIBWA

ROACH SPREADERS

G.W.

The artisan cut a gorget from a curved marine shell and engraved the concave, or inner, surface. Since the shells often were only a little more than three inches wide, the work required great skill. The only tools he used were sharp stones.

The gorget illustrated on the left shows a strong Mexican influence. The one on the right has a squared scroll topped with heads of the ivory-billed woodpecker.

3
WOOD AND STONE

Wood and stone were available in nearly every part of the country, and the Indians put these materials to good use.

The Iroquois, of New York and Canada, carved utensils from wood with great skill. The handles on their spoons were curved to fit over the rim of a bowl or kettle, so the spoon would not slip into the food. Birds and animals, often representing the owner's

29

clan totem, were favored for the carvings on them. The ones illustrated show a grouse, a woodcock, and a human figure. Ceremonial spoons belonged to individuals and were brought to longhouse festivals.

Maple-sugar utensils, including ladles and stirrers, were decorated, often with cutout designs. These stirrers also were used in tribal ceremonies such as the Strawberry Festival and for stirring the soup in the Green Corn Ceremony. The Indians boiled the finished utensils in a dye made from hemlock bark to give them a warm, dark color.

Some of the finest examples of Iroquois wood carving were the many grotesque masks that the members of the False Face Society wore during special functions. These masks, which were varied in design, represented mythological and legendary characters.

One was called crooked face. According to the Iroquois, he was hit in the face with a mountain, causing the twisted expression, because he showed disrespect for the Great Spirit. The doctor, or medicine, mask was very powerful. Supposedly when a great storm was nearing a village, he could blow it

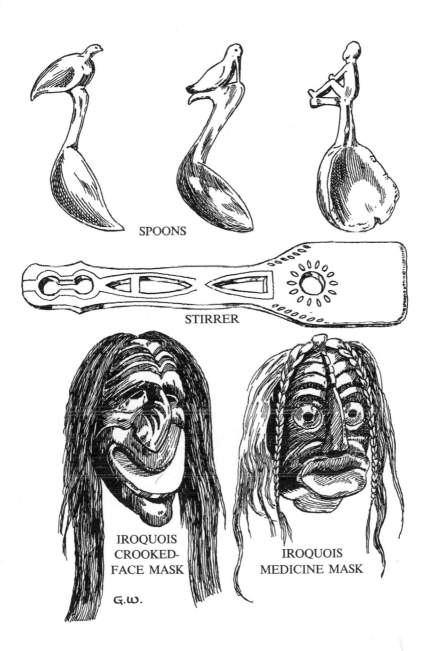

SPOONS

STIRRER

IROQUOIS
CROOKED-
FACE MASK

IROQUOIS
MEDICINE MASK

G.W.

away. The large lips on the mask account for this ability.

Most of the masks were painted either red or black, though some, called cousin masks, were half red, half black, with the dividing line running vertically through the center.

The Cherokee, of North Carolina, who were close relatives of the Iroquois, also had masks called booger masks, but they were not as well made and rarely were painted. The ones illustrated represent a pig and a cow.

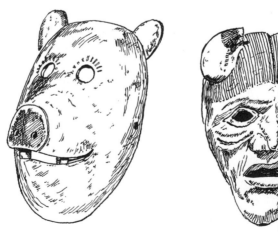

Of the many Indian peoples, however, the Northwest Coast Indians may have been the best carvers of all. Well-known as they were for their totem poles, they also made most of their personal and ceremonial objects. All of these, even such everyday items as the halibut fishhooks, were highly carved with designs representing human figures, birds, and animals. Some also were painted.

Their ceremonial masks varied in size and shape. Some were actually two masks in one. They were constructed so that when the wearer pulled certain

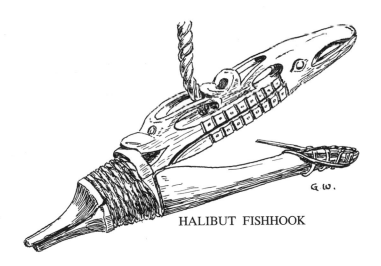

HALIBUT FISHHOOK

cords, the outer mask opened up, revealing an additional face on each side. Bird masks with very large beaks had hinges on them, and the beak could be opened wide by pulling on cords.

The ceremonies during which the masks were worn usually were conducted at night within the large plank houses. Thus, deep shadows created by the central fire lighting up the room prevented the audience from seeing the telltale cords. The carvings of birds and animals on the masks were large and grotesque, created purposely to frighten onlookers watching the performances of the shamans, or medicine men.

Ceremonial rattles also differed in shape and design. Some, known as moon rattles, were globular and had a face carved on each half. Certain medicine rattles were fine pieces of wood sculpture with delicate figures of men, frogs, and fish carved in high relief.

Food bowls and bowls holding oil into which the food was dipped often had facing lips, which were beautifully carved with gouged-out designs or realis-

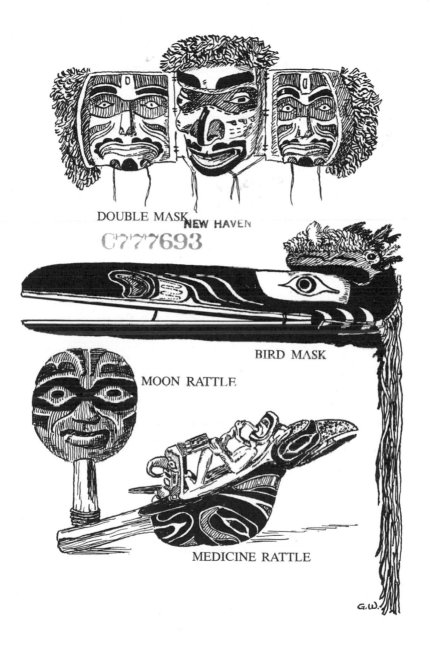

DOUBLE MASK

BIRD MASK

MOON RATTLE

MEDICINE RATTLE

G.W.

tic figures. Sometimes abalone shells were inserted into the eyes and ears of a figure. Mortars, in which ceremonial tobacco was ground, also had carvings on them.

Among some tribes, the leaders of the village wore wooden hats or helmets. The top of a typical one made by the Haida Indians in Alaska represented an eagle. It was inlaid with shell and had a fringe of human hair at the back.

The Chilkat, of British Columbia, made a hat with shell inlays in the ears and eyes of a figure. This hat had cylinders of woven basketry stacked on top, each cylinder representing a potlatch given by the owner. The wearer of the hat that is illustrated must have been a man of great wealth to have given eight such great feasts. The figure on the hat shows that he was a member of the wolf clan.

Another type of clan headdress had a crown of buckskin, which was decorated with feathers and was held upright with the stiff whiskers from a sea otter. A trailer, also of buckskin, hung down in back to the wearer's waist and was decorated with white

TOBACCO MORTAR

HAIDA HELMET
WITH EAGLE

CHILKAT HAT
WITH BASKET TOP

G.W.

ermine skins. The carved frontal ornament was either a flat mask resting on the wearer's forehead or a full animal mask fastened at the sides of the crown, extending forward.

The chiefs carried highly carved ceremonial staffs to show their importance. The leader of the whale hunters had a staff carved with a whale emblem. The leaders of the songs owned taller staffs, which also were painted.

Ceremonial masks as well as clothing were stored in large wooden boxes, made from a long piece of wood. First the craftsman cut three notches across the board, dividing it into four sections. Then he steamed the wood and folded it to form a container. Next he stitched the sides of the box together with cords made from twisted inner bark from the cedar. He also sewed a bottom onto the box and finally added a fitted lid. The entire box was beautifully carved and often had inlays of abalone shell pieces or cowrie shells.

Carving also was done in the Southwest, although not nearly to the same extent. The Hopi Indians,

living in the center of Navaho country in Arizona, were the creators of the fine, carved kachina dolls. Although theirs were the best known, other pueblos, such as the Zuñi and even the Navaho, made them too.

There were approximately 250 different dolls, representing everything from birds, animals, and reptiles to beans, squash, melon, and corn. Some, known as mudheads, were clowns.

These figures, which were replicas of the real kachina dancers that took part in the village ceremonies, were revered as a link between gods and

KACHINA DANCERS

mortals. During the year the dancers made the small carved and painted dolls in the seclusion of the underground kiva. At the end of the actual dances, they presented them to the little girls of the village. The dolls were hung on the adobe wall or were suspended from a roof beam. They served as a means of educating the children about the full function and meaning of each kachina.

The dolls had a stiff, blocklike appearance. Those illustrated represent a badger, a brown-and-yellow lizard, and a kachina maiden. In this dance the female is impersonated by a man.

Smoking was a ceremonial activity among nearly all the tribes. Thus, there were pipes of many styles.

Most pipestems were made of wood. They were either flat or tubular and were decorated with quill-work, horsehair, and feathers. Some flat stems had animal figures carved on them in relief.

The Sioux had a flat, broad pipestem called the puzzle stem. To make it, the Indian cut two rows of slits in pairs all along the piece of wood. Then he split it lengthwise and gouged out the smoke channel, zigzagging it in and around the rows of slits. Lastly he glued the two halves together again.

The Sioux also made a pipestem that was twisted like rope. Every twist was carved to a uniform size.

Some pipebowls were made from quartzite and other hard rock. The Iroquois used pipes with a bowl and stem of baked clay. Most bowls, however, were made from the sacred red pipestone.

Although deposits of this stone could be found in several states, a number of tribes traveled many miles to obtain it from the quarries in southeastern Minnesota. According to legend, the stone was colored by

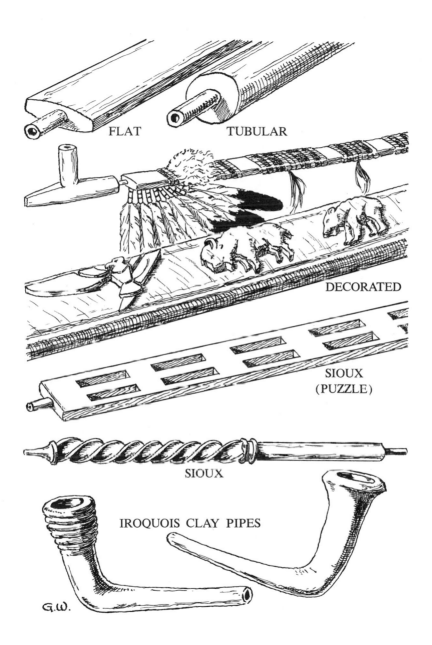

FLAT   TUBULAR

DECORATED

SIOUX
(PUZZLE)

SIOUX

IROQUOIS CLAY PIPES

G.W.

the blood of warring tribes. Finally the Great Spirit appeared to them on that site and told them that from that moment on, whenever the tribes congregated there, they had to meet as friends and brothers. The most common pipebowls were shaped like an inverted letter *T*. Often they were ornamented with raised rings around the upper part of the bowl and near the end where the stem was inserted. Some pipemakers, however, cut designs into the bowls and filled the hollows with lead. When the pipe was polished with oil, the shining lead made a pleasing contrast to the red pipestone.

L-shaped bowls were common among several tribes, although there were slight variations. The Blackfeet preferred a black stone pipe with an acorn-shaped bowl.

Many of the warrior societies among the Plains Indians had ceremonial pipes with carvings attached to the bowl or a carved design worked on the bowl itself.

The pipes with carved figures on them were called effigy pipes. Some featured a standing buffalo, its

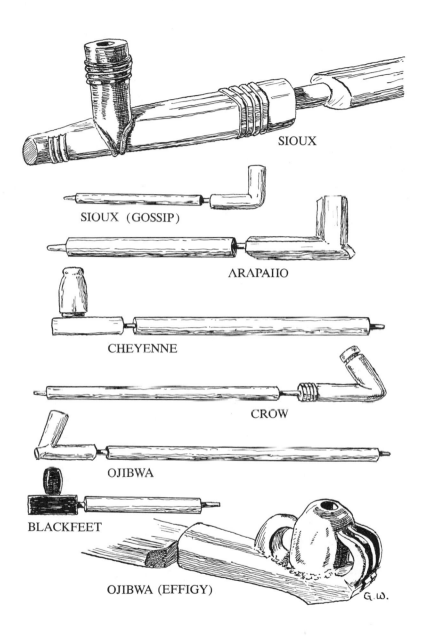

SIOUX

SIOUX (GOSSIP)

ARAPAHO

CHEYENNE

CROW

OJIBWA

BLACKFEET

OJIBWA (EFFIGY)

G.W.

head toward the bowl, or a wolf, either standing or squatting. Others even had a human figure resting against the bowl. One pipe, made by the Ojibwa, represented an acorn held in the talons of an eagle. The hollowed-out acorn was the actual bowl.

A society known as the White Buffalo Society, which honored the rare white, or albino, buffalo, had a pipe that was smoked only during ceremonials of great importance. The bowl was flat and broad, and in the center of the broadest part was a shallow well for the tobacco. On the flat wooden stem were carved the imprints of buffalo hoofs.

The Mound Builders, of Ohio, made the most beautiful and artistic effigy pipes. The stone birds and human figures were as skillfully carved as ornamental sculpture pieces.

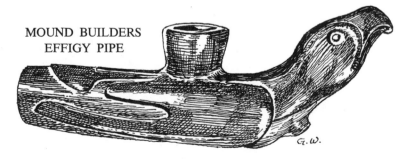

MOUND BUILDERS
EFFIGY PIPE

WHITE BUFFALO SOCIETY
CEREMONIAL PIPE

G.W.

4
ROOTS, TWIGS, AND GRASSES

Basket making is one of the oldest arts. It is thought to have originated as an imitation of the way birds build their nests. There are few, if any, Indian tribes who did not weave baskets of some sort. They served as storage and cooking vessels, and, among some Indians, as baby cradles.

The styles of basketry among the different tribes could be identified not only by the materials used,

48

but by the weaving technique and design. The fact that so many tribes made baskets accounts for their great diversity.

Much time and skill went into the construction of a good basket. The weaver had to know in what season to gather her materials and how to harvest, dry, preserve, and prepare them for her use. She also had to master the intricate techniques required.

Over the centuries many tribes improved this skill. However, among the Ojibwa and Menomini of the Northwest, basketry was not strongly developed, primarily because they used birchbark for their containers, but they also made some small, shallow baskets for a favorite gambling game. In this game, the Indians tossed marked sticks, bone pieces, or wild-plum pits into the container, somewhat the way men throw dice today.

The Indians of the Northwest Coast made baskets from twined split spruce roots and embroidered them with colored grasses. Many of these coastal tribes wore high-crowned basketry hats with their well-known totemic designs painted on them. These were said to be the most elaborately painted of all Indian basketry.

The tribes of the Southwest had a particularly wide range of designs. One group of Hopi produced wickerwork baskets. Although this type of weave was unusual among the American Indians, it was one of the finest and most artistic in the world.

In this work the warp, or foundation, consisted of a number of sumac or willow twigs radiating from a central hub. The weft, or weaving material, was obtained from rabbit brush. To make a mat, the weaver interlaced the weft with the warp in ever-increasing circles. Since the radiating spokes were spread farther apart toward the ends, the weaver filled the spaces in between with more twigs. The mat, therefore, had more spokes at the outer rim than the center. The weaver finished the piece by bending the spoke ends over and then firmly wrapping them in place.

The brush used for the weaving was dyed with mineral colors and formed pleasing designs. Some of these designs were a geometric or whirlwind pat-

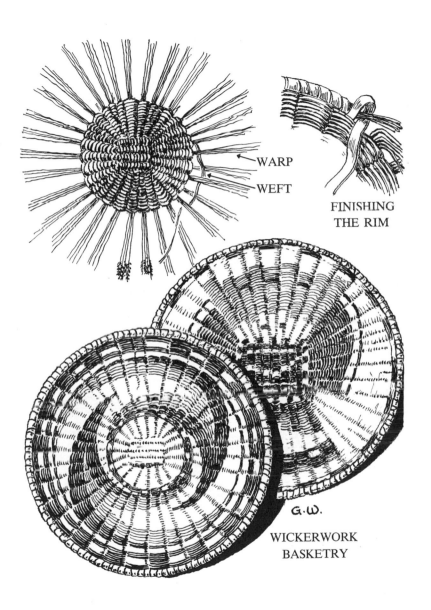

WARP

WEFT

FINISHING
THE RIM

G.W.

WICKERWORK
BASKETRY

tern, but in most instances they were kachinas, kachina masks, or life forms, such as birds and butterflies.

Flat or slightly curved trays woven in this way held food or the sacred cornmeal used in the blessing rites during the ceremonies. Straight-sided woven baskets were used for storage.

The Hopi and the many other Pueblo villages also made coiled baskets. The foundation was constructed from strands of coarse grass, which the weaver wrapped in strips of yucca leaves. As she coiled the wrapped grass, she sewed the coil onto the preceding one by passing the yucca strip through a hole made

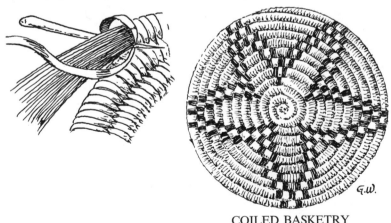

COILED BASKETRY

with a bone awl. She pulled each stitch tight, binding the coils together firmly. Flat as well as slightly concave trays were made in this manner, as well as globular baskets with lids, in which seeds were stored.

One fine example of the Navaho craft was the wedding basket. The opening in the star-shaped design is said to have been an escape route for the maker's soul, preventing it from becoming ensnared in the weave, or as an exit for any bad thoughts the weaver might have had while working. The oldest types of these baskets had flaring sides and were thirty inches wide and ten inches deep.

NAVAHO WEDDING BASKET   NAVAHO HOGAN

Among the Apache there were baskets formed like clay pots. Still others were shaped like narrow, tall-necked bottles. Designs on these baskets often consisted of several parallel lines in a zigzag pattern, which was placed vertically or horizontally. On their flat food trays, the patterns started at the center and spread to the outer rim. Still other decorations showed isolated figures of people and animals, diamond shapes, and crosses.

Some woven jars were covered with pitch from the piñon pine to make them watertight. Burden baskets shaped like large cones were decorated with buckskin fringes along the rim, down the sides, and hanging from the bottom.

The Papago, of southern Arizona, produced coiled baskets that were quite unlike those of other tribes. They were made of bear grass, and instead of being wrapped, the grass was held together at regular intervals with a split stitch, which also served as the design. This type of stitch was made from a combination of bleached yucca leaves and the black outer covering of devil's-claw seed pods.

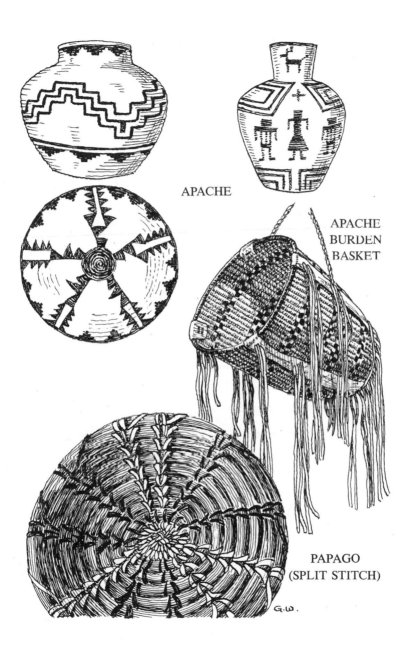

APACHE

APACHE
BURDEN
BASKET

PAPAGO
(SPLIT STITCH)

G.W.

5
CLAY

Most of the nomadic tribes did not practice the art of pottery making, since transporting clay pots on a travois resulted in too many broken pieces. Also, the woodland people preferred to use birchbark for their cooking and storage needs. The Iroquois, however, made some clay pots, often with a pointed bottom, so they could stand firmly in hot ashes.

The outstanding potters were the Indians of the

Southwest, where pottery was invented by the prehistoric people, the Basket Makers, about sixteen
hundred years ago. Around 1690, the Pueblo Indians
began to develop different styles, so that eventually
the village in which a piece was made could be
identified.

The food bowls were somewhat shallow and wide.
Cooking pots of the Papago often had flat side
handles for easy lifting. Taller jars were formed so
they spread wide at or above the middle, then tapered
toward the top rim. The tallest and most graceful
were those made at the Zia pueblo. The Maricopa
made long, slender-necked jars.

Some villages produced a double-necked wedding
jar. During the wedding ceremony the bride and
groom drank from it together.

Undecorated ware was used for cooking, while
decorated pieces were used for storage of seeds and
grain and for carrying water. The women carried
the large water jars on their heads by balancing them
in a specially made basketry ring in the form of a
bottomless, round basket.

ZIA   ACOMA   JEMEZ

LAGUNA   HOPI   SAN JUAN

MARICOPA   ZUÑI   PAPAGO (FOOD)

TAOS (BEAN)   SANTO DOMINGO

In 1958, through the combined efforts of the National Geographic Society and the National Park Service, pottery made by the early Cliff Dwellers more than seven hundred years ago was discovered at Mesa Verde National Park, in Colorado. The excavations uncovered food bowls and pitchers. This discovery gives evidence where these early people, who eventually moved south into Arizona and New Mexico, came from.

A story is told about the origin of pottery making. Some tribes made waterproof jars by smearing baskets with pitch. In other pueblos, however, the women coated their baskets with clay instead.

One day a woman left her clay-covered basket too close to her cooking fire, with the result that the heat from it caused the clay to bake hard. Then she experimented further, and after some trial and error she finally produced a watertight clay container without a basket foundation.

The gathering of clay for pottery making was often a festive affair. Families and friends went together on such an outing. Arriving at one of the clay beds close to the village, they gathered the clay, which was found in slabs and chunks of all sizes. They also collected fine sand from the riverbanks and brought it home with the clay.

Back at the village, the clay was broken up, pounded, and ground on a stone slab until it was as fine as mill-ground flour. In the grinding process all stones and other foreign matter were carefully removed and discarded. The fine sand was washed in a basket to rid it of unwanted pebbles.

With very few exceptions the potter was a woman. First she mixed the clay and sand, which was a delicate operation, requiring skill. If the mixture had too much clay, the vessel would crack in baking or be too porous. If it had too much sand, it would crumble.

Placing two parts of clay to one part of sand on a piece of cloth, the potter blended them together thoroughly with her hands. After sprinkling water over the mixture until it was fairly moist, she kneaded, patted, and rolled it like dough. If necessary, she again spread it out and added more water.

The amount of water was also important. If there was too much, the pot collapsed as it dried. If there was too little, it did not stick together.

The only tools the potter used were gourd pieces of different shapes. She kept her hands moist at all times by dipping them frequently in water. She used as a base the bottom of a broken piece of pottery, a gourd section, or a saucer, which she turned freely while she worked.

To make a pot, first the woman kneaded and patted a piece of the clay to fit over the base. Then she rolled a small amount of clay into a rounded strip and placed it around the edge of the bottom piece. After pressing it into place, she smoothed it with a piece of dried gourd. Then she pressed another coil on top of the first and smoothed it. She added more coils in the same manner. As the vessel was built, the potter thinned the walls in the process.

Once the pot was completed, she set it aside to dry, first in the shade and later in the sun. Then she scraped it, often with a piece of glass, to smooth the sides. Finally she added several coats of a slip with a rabbit's tail. This was a thin mixture of colored clay and water, which created a monochrome background and a good surface for a painted design.

Then the pot was ready for painting. Paintbrushes were made from pieces of stems from the yucca plant. The pulp was removed from one end, and the remaining fibers formed the brush.

The artist painted all her designs freehand, without even the use of guidelines. She was so skilled in this art, and so accurate in her planning of the design, that when she finally painted around to the point on the pot where she had started, the design was perfectly spaced out. She made the large designs first and outlined broad lines or solid patterns, filling them in later.

After the painting was dry, the potter prepared to fire the pot. She built a fire in a place where it was sheltered from the wind and left it to burn to coals. Then she placed stones about equal size in the coals and laid thin slabs of stone across them.

She set the pot, upside down, on this platform, taking care that it did not touch other vessels. Next

the potter covered it with large pieces of old, broken pottery, called shards, to prevent the flames from touching the clay, which would produce dark spots. Finally she spread a layer of dry sheep manure over the pile, leaving a few openings to permit circulation of air and heat.

The potter pushed kindling under the stone grate and lit it. If properly made, the fire burned for nearly two hours, reaching temperatures from twelve to fifteen hundred degrees Fahrenheit.

When the firing was done, the potter removed the pot from the ashes with sticks and placed it nearby to cool. Lastly, she dusted off the ashes with a dry cloth.

6

COPPER AND SILVER

The first metal the American Indians used for the making of tools, weapons, and ornaments was native copper. Some was mined locally, while in other places it was found in nugget form, where it had been deposited during the glacial periods. Some glacial deposits, called float copper, were found in the Southwest, but work with this metal was not highly developed in that region.

The Indians of New England, New Jersey, and nearby states possessed copper, as well as those in the Great Lakes and the Mississippi Valley. The Indians along the Northwest coastal areas and in southeastern Alaska were perhaps the greatest users of this metal.

Certainly their shieldlike ornaments known as coppers were the largest art forms. These hammered, and sometimes, painted pieces, usually about two and one-half feet high, were symbols of a man's high position in the village. They were hung on the walls of a house. During a potlatch given for a rival chief, a man might destroy several of them to demonstrate that he was so wealthy their loss was of no importance to him.

To make the copper, the craftsman pounded the metal flat with a stone. At times, he heated it first to make it less brittle and tougher. To cut out the shape, he hammered grooves along a prescratched outline, creating a sharp ridge on the reverse side. Then he turned the copper over and rubbed the ridge with a piece of sandstone until it was cut through.

CUT   BEND

RUBBING TO CUT RIDGE

COPPERS

Next he hammered the bent-up edges flat. For decoration, he cut grooves into the metal from the front and hammered raised patterns into it from the back.

In the seventeenth century the French and Dutch in New York introduced silver and the metallic instruments for working it to the Iroquois. At first silver was obtained by melting down silver dollars or Mexican silver coins, but after this practice was prohibited, the traders introduced sheet or ingot silver. Learning from the white silversmith, the Iroquois soon became the leading makers of silver jewelry. Almost every village had its own smith.

A great change in ornamental work took place with the introduction of German silver, also known as nickel silver. An alloy of copper, nickel, and zinc, it was more durable and less costly than true silver.

The Iroquois copied pins and brooches from the early European designs, and these became the most popular silver ornaments. They were used to fasten garments and decorated the costumes of both men and women. They adorned sashes, headbands, as well as the wide broadcloth bands on cradleboards.

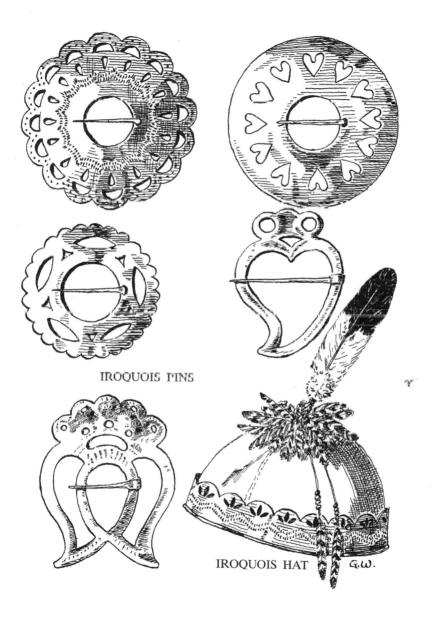

IROQUOIS PINS

IROQUOIS HAT   G.W.

Since German silver was quite thin, the craftsman made the openwork and engraved designs on the ornament while it was still flat. Then he placed it over a slightly rounded block of wood and hammered it into a convex shape.

The decorated buckskin or cloth band fastened around the edge of the Iroquois hat, or *gustoweh,* was discarded for a broad silver band with engravings and cutout designs. With the coming of the Jesuits, in 1654, the Iroquois also made silver crosses, but they were worn simply as ornaments rather than for any religious purpose.

In the course of trade between tribes, the art of silverwork spread out from the Great Lakes region to the north and through the Southeast during the period from 1800 to 1860. By 1810, it also had reached the Great Plains, and there the styles gradually changed to conform with the art forms of the tribes in those areas.

Since the turn of the century, a great influence in the art of the Plains silverwork has been the peyote cult and the Native American Church. This cult

followed the Ghost Dance, which was performed
from 1888 to 1890, as one of the last great native
religious movements, and in practice it was one of
prayers and meditation.

Peyote jewelry was ornamented with designs of
spirit birds, crescent shapes, drums, fans, rattles, and
tepees, all of which figured in the ceremonies and
rituals. Such articles as earrings, stickpins, and neckerchief holders often were worn during meetings of
the Church members, although the jewelry itself was
not actually a part of the ritual.

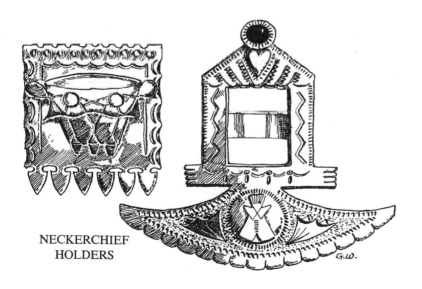

NECKERCHIEF
HOLDERS

The Kiowa Indians called German silver "flat metal." Although they claim to have obtained it in 1866, very likely it was traded to them as early as 1850. This tribe made bridle ornaments from the metal. A warrior often wore a leather streamer decorated with convex silver disks, or conchas, tied to the back of his hair.

The Arapaho, especially the women, wore silver-ornamented belts with a long, tapering piece of leather hanging down in front. This piece was decorated with still more conchas, which were graduated in size to conform with the taper.

The silverwork of the Navaho Indians is widely known today. Although many people think that it was an ancient art of these Indians, actually they did not learn it until the late 1850s. At that time Mexican smiths wandered through Navaho country making silver ornaments in exchange for horses.

The Navaho borrowed from these early designs, many of which came from Spain and had a Moorish origin. Their silver buttons, hollow beads, silver-mounted bridles, and the squash blossom necklaces

ARAPAHO

KIOWA WARRIOR

G.W.

were adaptations from the Spanish. This blossom originally ornamented the trouser seams and capes of Spanish gentlemen. The Navaho did not regard the crescent-shaped pendant on these necklaces as a good-luck charm as the Spaniards did.

The Navaho also copied the bracelets, rings, and concha belts of the Plains Indians, which they obtained through trade with the Utes, Kiowas, and Comanches.

The earliest pieces of Navaho jewelry were not set with turquoise. Then, between 1880 and 1885, a few stone-set pieces were made. These are now very rare. Turquoise was not used extensively until about 1900.

Around 1870, both the Zuñi and the Hopi made silverwork much like that of the Navaho. By 1890, the Zuñi began to add turquoise in multiple rows on bracelets and in clusters on pins and rings. In 1935, they also were setting jet and shell on their jewelry to such an extent that the inlay nearly hid the silver.

In 1938, the Hopi began to develop a new style in silverwork based on their distinctive pottery designs. In this work two pieces of silver were combined. The

NAVAHO

ZUÑI

NAVAHO
CONCHA BELT

ZUÑI PIN

ZUÑI PENDANT

HOPI
OVERLAY
PIN

NAVAHO
SQUASH BLOSSOM
NECKLACE

G.W.

craftsman cut the design out of the top piece with a jeweler's saw. Then he overlaid it on a solid flat piece of the same size and shape and bound the two together with a torch, in a process called sweating. Finally he blackened the bottom piece with a coating of liver of sulfur, so that the design stood out. The craftsmanship was so fine the jewelry appeared to have been made from a single, carved piece of silver.

The workshop of the Southwestern silversmith was quite simple. It contained a crude forge in which he burned charcoal of his own making, a crucible, or container, of hard-baked clay in which the silver was melted, and a set of handmade bellows to keep the coals alive.

His anvil was a smooth rock. The tools he used most often were thongs and pliers, small files, awls, and cold chisels. He made dies and stamps on pieces of metal, usually old files.

In addition to making hand-hammered jewelry, the silversmith sand-casted some pieces. The mold in which the jewelry was formed was fashioned from soft volcanic pumice. The Indian ground one side

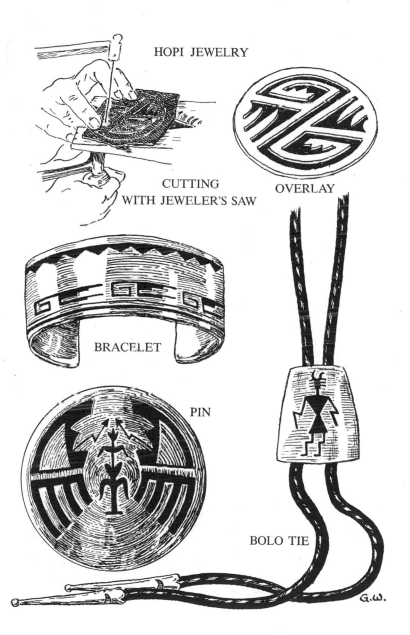

HOPI JEWELRY

CUTTING
WITH JEWELER'S SAW

OVERLAY

BRACELET

PIN

BOLO TIE

G.W.

smooth, and then cut the desired design into it with a knife. At one end he left an opening in which to pour the melted silver. He also cut channels leading from the design to the outer edges to prevent air pockets from forming.

The smith smoked the mold, so that the silver would flow freely over the carbonized covering. Then he placed a flat slab of pumice, also smoked, on top of the carved block, wired them together, and poured the silver, which had been melted in the crucible, into the mold. The casting was quite rough, so the smith finished the piece by filing and polishing it.

Bracelets made in this manner were cast flat and later were shaped by hammering.

CHANNELS TO PREVENT
AIR POCKETS

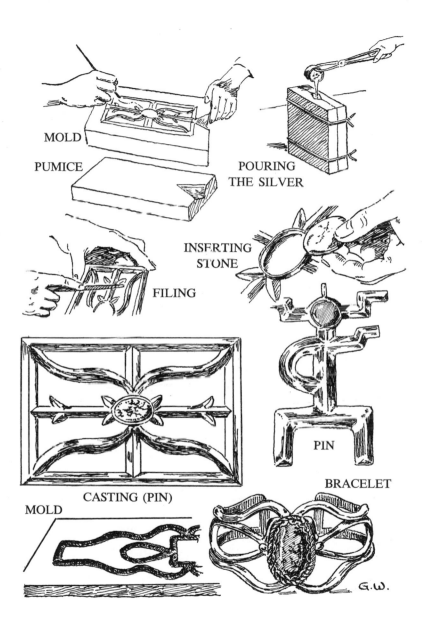

MOLD

PUMICE

POURING
THE SILVER

INSERTING
STONE

FILING

CASTING (PIN)

PIN

BRACELET

MOLD

G.W.

7

INDIAN ARTS TODAY

Many early examples of Indian art have been lost. The white settlers were not interested in preserving any of the Indian's crafts, and missionaries demanded that all work made by heathens be destroyed. In addition, many articles made from wood and skin have been ruined by climatic conditions.

Early white artists, such as George Catlin, were among the first to value the Indian's art, and they began to collect items from the tribes they visited. Fortunately others, too, recognized its worth, and today there are fine Indian collections in our large museums. Some of them exhibit the artifacts of many tribes, while others are limited to those of the local Indians.

There was a time, however, when the art of the Indian deteriorated, partly because he had no outlet for his best work. To satisfy the tourist demand, he created unauthentic kachina dolls, cheap pottery painted in bright poster colors, narrow, stamped bracelets with figures that told a story, as well as Navaho rugs in gaudy colors.

Then people began to appreciate the Indian's art, and the interest in quality workmanship gave new inspiration to artists in many fields. Reservation traders and other individuals helped some of the young painters sell their works. Museums held exhibitions of their paintings and offered prizes for the best ones. In 1932, the Bureau of Indian Affairs established a program in painting at the Santa Fe Indian School, and the paintings created there soon found a ready market both in this country and abroad.

As interest in Indian arts grew, the Indian Arts and Crafts Board of the United States Department of the Interior founded, in 1962, the Institute of American Indian Arts, also at Santa Fe. In addition, the Board has created an outlet for the Indian by setting up regional craft centers and shops in their Indian museums.

Today a number of fine artists from the West and the Southwest have become well-known for their individual styles. Their earliest subjects were ceremonial dancers, and they were executed in a two-dimensional, opaque watercolor technique. In time, their work began to show a better sense of composition and pictured their old legends, as well as daily life.

Several artists have used this two-dimensional style to great advantage in the creation of large murals, some of which can be seen in schools, museums, and Government buildings, such as post offices. A fine example of such mural work is repro-

RIO GRANDE
PUEBLO

BASKET DANCER

CORN DANCER

G.W.

duced on the jacket of this book. It is a detail of a
large painting of nineteenth-century Blackfeet life.
Painted in 1941 by Victor Pepion, a young Blackfeet, it is on view in the lobby gallery of the Museum
of the Plains Indian and Crafts Center at Browning,
Montana.

Another fine mural called "A Successful Raid," in
the Southern Plains Indian Exhibit and Crafts Center,
at Anadarko, Oklahoma, was painted by the Apache,
Allan Houser. Mr. Houser created paintings for several years, but during World War II he became interested in sculpture. Now several of his diorama
figures can be seen in the museum at Anadarko. Today he devotes most of his time to this art form,
working in marble, ebony, limestone, and mahogany.

In jewelry making, the Indian is exploring how to
use the old materials in new ways. A representative
piece is the charming pendant in the form of a
salmon illustrated here. It is made of elk antler with
abalone shell inlay. The other fish pendant is of
carved and incised caribou hoof.

Members of the Native American Church use

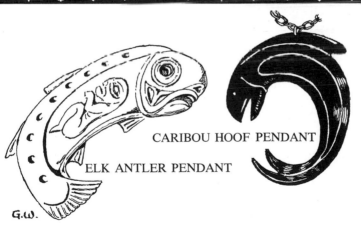

CARIBOU HOOF PENDANT

ELK ANTLER PENDANT

G.W.

jewelry of German silver. The most common religious symbol found in peyote jewelry is the aquatic
spirit bird. Usually it is depicted with neck extended
and wings open in flight. The tail feathers are made
either in one piece or are attached separately. In the
illustration, the peyote designs of the fan and the
spirit bird appear on a neckerchief holder.

Rings, bracelets, and cuff links are also made from
German silver. The long, linked silver earrings that
are fashionable today have their origin in the dentalium earrings worn by Indian women in the past.
The roach spreader with a linked pendant and socket
for a single feather is a copy of the earlier ones made
from bone.

Navaho jewelry has long been worn by non-Indian
women. The fine silver bracelets, buttons, necklaces,
and the large concha belts all lend themselves well
to modern styles.

The Zuñi and Hopi still make much of their silverwork for their own use, but in the last few years their
work has become popular with other people too.
Butterfly pins, necklaces, earrings, bolo ties, and

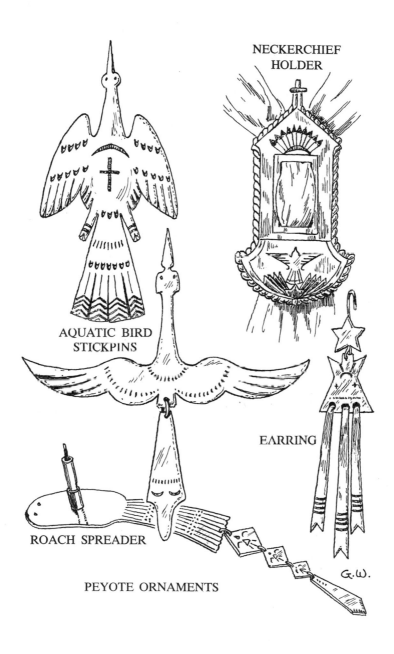

NECKERCHIEF
HOLDER

AQUATIC BIRD
STICKPINS

EARRING

ROACH SPREADER

PEYOTE ORNAMENTS

G.W.

turquoise-studded bracelets are among the favorite items. The fine overlay work of the Hopi is used for cuff links, belt buckles, silver boxes, and very attractive watchbands, some of which are set with a single turquoise on an oxidized background.

A revival of woodcarving was started at Haines, Alaska, in the 1940s, and it included the making of old-form masks, decorative carved panels, and other art forms.

Another item of Indian art in demand among collectors is the doll. In the last few years the so-called dancer doll came into being. Made from buckskin, over a wire foundation, it is dressed in typical beaded costume and has a roach on its head and a dance bustle at the back. Some even wear a small warbonnet. The doll stands on a wooden platform and can be bent to assume a dance position. The one that is illustrated was made by a Shoshoni Indian woman and was a prize winner at one of the Intertribal Ceremonies at Gallup, New Mexico.

The kachina dolls of the Southwest, such as the eagle dancers and the animal kachinas, also are real-

istic and show movement. Hopi mudhead kachinas and their counterpart, the Zuñi Koshare, are made to show them climbing poles.

On the Cherokee reservation in North Carolina, in the Smoky Mountains, basket making and other crafts are continuing, and many fine objects are sold at the craft center there.

Pottery still is being produced in the Southwest. Only about eighteen groups make the decorated ware, but undecorated cooking pots are made in nearly all the villages. The beautiful, highly polished, black or red pottery of the pueblos of San Ildefonso and Santa Clara in New Mexico has a background in a matte finish, which sets off the designs. In both these places pottery with deeply carved designs became popular in 1920. In this work the recessed designs also are set off with the dull background.

The old and the new Indian crafts are found to be well suited for modern home decoration. In the living room, the den, or a child's room, one or more Navaho rugs create warmth and color. A pair of kachina dolls hung on the wall or standing on the

SAN ILDEFONSO

SANTA CLARA

SAN ILDEFONSO

G.W.

SANTA CLARA

mantel, or a fine piece of pottery on a bookshelf, adds much charm to a room. A painting made by an Indian artist has an interesting subject, and its soft earth colors blend with almost any decor. Large baskets, serving as wastebaskets, are a unique touch, and since those from different tribes rarely clash, they may be mixed in the same room.

People today are gaining a greater awareness of the value of Indian arts. The contemporary Indian artist is making an important contribution to our modern culture by keeping alive many of the traditions of the past.

INDEX

Indicates illustration

Robert Hofsinde was born in Denmark, where he received his formal education as well as his art training. In his late teens he came to the United States and settled in northern Minnesota. While trapping there one winter, he saved the life of a Chippewa Indian boy, and in gratitude the Chippewa made him a blood brother of the tribe, giving him the name Gray-Wolf. This contact led him to a profound interest in the culture of the Indian, and in the years that followed he engaged in comprehensive research among many different tribes. Today he is a recognized authority in the field. An author of many books on Indian lore, he is often asked to give lectures and to make TV appearances. He and his wife live in Orange County, New York.